Pleasures of the Heart

To _____

From _____

Copyright © 1995 by Garborg's Heart 'n Home, Inc.

Published by Garborg's Heart 'n Home, Inc.
P.O. Box 20132, Bloomington, MN 55420

Illustrations © 1995 by Stephen Whittle.
All rights reserved.
ISBN 1-881830-15-2

$\mathcal{S}$ee each morning a world made anew, as if it were the morning of the very first day;... treasure and use it, as if it were the final hour of the very last day.

FAY HARTZELL ARNOLD

$\mathcal{T}$ime...is a sacred gift, and each day is a little life.

JOHN LUBBOCK

*J*oys come from simple and natural things: mists over meadows, sunlight on leaves, the path of the moon over water.

SIGURD F. OLSON

*A*s a countenance is made beautiful by the soul's shining through it, so the world is beautiful by the shining through it of God.

FRIEDRICH HEINRICH JACOBI

*W*hen we call on God, he bends down his ear to listen, as a father bends down to listen to his little child.

ELIZABETH CHARLES

I love the Lord because he hears my prayers and answers them. Because he bends down and listens, I will pray as long as I breathe!

PSALM 116:1,2 TLB

$\mathcal{W}$e can make up our
minds whether our lives in
this world shall...be beautiful and
fragrant like the lilies of the field.

FATHER ANDREW SDC

The path of the righteous is like the light
of dawn, which shines brighter and
brighter until full day.

PROVERBS 4:18 NRSV

$\mathcal{L}$ook for the heaven here on earth. It is all around you.

$\mathcal{T}$he joyful birds prolong the strain,
Their song with every spring
   renewed;
The air we breathe, and
   falling rain,
Each softly whispers:
   God is good.

JOHN HAMPDEN GURNEY

The Lord bless you and
keep you;
The Lord make His face
shine upon you,
And be gracious to you;
The Lord lift up His countenance upon you
And give you peace.

Numbers 6:24-26 NKJV

If we had no winter, the spring would not be so pleasant; if we did not sometimes taste of adversity, prosperity would not be so welcome.

ANNE BRADSTREET

*A*fter winter comes the summer. After night comes the dawn. And after every storm, there comes clear, open skies.

SAMUEL RUTHERFORD

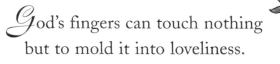

*G*od's fingers can touch nothing
but to mold it into loveliness.

GEORGE MACDONALD

*G*od puts each fresh morning, each new
chance of life, into our hands as a gift
to see what we will do with it.

$\mathcal{A}$ll the things in this world are gifts and signs of God's love to us. The whole world is a love letter from God.

PETER KREEFT

$\mathcal{H}$e surrounds me with lovingkindness and tender mercies. He fills my life with good things.

PSALM 103:4,5 TLB

Our joy will be complete
if we remain in his love —
for his love is personal,
intimate, real, living,
delicate, faithful love.

MOTHER TERESA

The earth is filled with his tender love.

PSALM 33:5 TLB

I lift up my eyes to the quiet hills,
And my heart to the Father's throne;
In all my ways, to the end of days,
The Lord will preserve his own.

TIMOTHY DUDLEY-SMITH

My help comes from the Lord,
who made heaven and earth.
He...will neither slumber
nor sleep.

PSALM 121:2,4 NRSV

Our Creator would never have
made such lovely days and have given
us the deep hearts to enjoy them, above
and beyond all thought, unless we
were meant to be immortal.

NATHANIEL HAWTHORNE

The well of Providence is deep. It's the buckets we bring to it that are small.

MARY WEBB

Just as there comes a warm sunbeam into every cottage window, so comes a love—born of God's care for every separate need.

NATHANIEL HAWTHORNE

The best memory is that which forgets nothing but injuries. Write kindness in marble and write injuries in the dust.

PERSIAN PROVERB

Be kind to one another, tenderhearted, forgiving one another, as God in Christ has forgiven you.

EPHESIANS 4:32 NRSV

Far away, there in the sunshine,
are my highest aspirations. I may
not reach them but I can look up
and see their beauty, believe in
them, and try to follow where
they lead.

LOUISA MAY ALCOTT

God's gifts put man's best
dreams to shame.

ELIZABETH BARRETT BROWNING

$\mathcal{T}$his I call to mind, and therefore
I have hope: The steadfast love of the
Lord never ceases, his mercies never
come to an end; they are new every
morning; great is your faithfulness.

LAMENTATIONS 3:22,23 NRSV

$\mathcal{L}$et there be many windows in your soul,
That all the glory of the universe may beautify it.

ELLA WHEELER WILCOX

$\mathcal{Y}$ours, O Lord, are the
greatness, the power, the glory,
the victory, and the majesty;
for all that is in heaven and
on the earth is yours.

1 CHRONICLES 29:11 NRSV

$\mathcal{G}$od is constantly taking
knowledge of me in love,
and watching over me for
my own good.

J. I. PACKER

$\mathcal{H}$ow precious is your constant love, O God!
All humanity takes refure in the shadow of
your wings.

PSALM 36:7 TLB

*W*hen I think upon my God,
my heart is so full of joy that the
notes dance and leap from my pen.

FRANZ JOSEPH HAYDN

*A*s for God, his way is perfect.

PSALM 18:30 KJV

*E*verything around me
may change, but our God
is changeless!

CAROL KENT

*T*his day is all that
is good and fair. It is too dear,
with its hopes and invitations, to
waste a moment on yesterdays.

RALPH WALDO EMERSON

*L*ife...gives you the chance to love,
to work, to play, and to look
up at the stars.

HENRY VAN DYKE

The beauty of the sunbeam lies partly in the fact that God does not keep it; he gives it away to us all.

DAVID SWING

Something deep in all of us yearns for God's beauty, and we can find it no matter where we are.

SUE MONK KIDD

$\mathcal{H}$eaven will be the endless portion of those who have heaven in their soul.

$\mathcal{Y}$ou will show me the path of life; in Your presence is fullness of joy; at Your right hand are pleasures forevermore.

PSALM 16:11 NKJV

The love of the Father is like a sudden rain shower that will pour forth when you least expect it, catching you up into wonder and praise.

RICHARD FOSTER

The Lord will...satisfy you with all good things...you will be like a well-watered garden, like an ever-flowing spring.

ISAIAH 58:11 TLB

$\mathcal{S}$omewhere on the great world
the sun is always shining, and just so
sure as you live, it will sometime shine
on you. The dear God made it so.
There is so much sunshine we
must all have our share.

MYRTLE REED

$\mathcal{G}$od did not make the first human because he needed company, but because he wanted someone to whom he could show his generosity and love.

IRENAEUS

$\mathcal{T}$he Lord, your God, is in your midst...he will renew you in his love; he will exult over you with loud singing.

ZEPHANIAH 3:17 NRSV

$\mathcal{T}$ake rest; a field that has rested gives a bountiful crop.

OVID

$\mathcal{L}$et us never lose sight of the reason for the journey, or miss a chance to see a rainbow on the way.

GLORIA GAITHER

*L*ife, like the waters of the seas, freshens only when it ascends to heaven.

JEAN PAUL RICHTER

*T*hey that wait upon the Lord shall renew their strength. They shall mount up with wings like eagles; they shall run and not be weary; they shall walk and not faint.

ISAIAH 40:31 TLB

$\mathcal{L}$ife is so full of meaning
and purpose, so full of beauty–
beneath its covering–that you will
find that earth but cloaks your heaven.

FRA GIOVANNI

$\mathcal{I}$nstead of seeking happiness by going
out of our place, our skill should be
to find it where we are.

HENRY WARD BEECHER

*F*aith goes up the stairs that love has made
and looks out of the windows which hope
has opened.

CHARLES H. SPURGEON

*F*aith makes all things
　　possible.
Hope makes all things bright.
Love makes all things easy.

$\mathcal{I}$t is God to whom and with whom we travel, and while he is the End of our journey, he is also at every stopping place.

ELISABETH ELLIOT

$\mathcal{I}$ am with you, and will protect you wherever you go.

GENESIS 28:15 TLB

It is only by thinking about great and good things that we come to love them, and it is only by loving them that we come to long for them, and it is only by longing for them that we are impelled to seek after them; and it is only by seeking after them that they become ours.

HENRY VAN DYKE

If I take the wings of the morning,
and settle at the farthest limits of the sea,
even there your hand shall lead me, and
your right hand shall hold me fast.

PSALM 139:9,10 NRSV

God knows no distance.

CHARLESZETTA WADDLES

$\mathcal{T}$o me, every hour of the day and night is an unspeakably perfect miracle.

WALT WHITMAN

$\mathcal{H}$alf the joy of life is in little things taken on the run. Let us run if we must—even the sands do that— but let us keep our hearts young and our eyes open that nothing worth our while shall escape us.

VICTOR CHERBULIEZ

$\mathscr{I}$ don't know what the future holds, but I know Who holds the future.

E. STANLEY JONES

$\mathscr{I}$ will be your God through all your lifetime....
I made you and I will care for you. I will carry
you along and be your Savior.

ISAIAH 46:4 TLB

*F*aith makes the uplook good,
the outlook bright, the inlook
favorable, and the future glorious.

V. RAYMOND EDMAN

*H*appy times and bygone days
are never lost.... In truth, they
grow more wonderful within
the heart that keeps them.

KAY ANDREW